What if we do
NOTHING?

THE OBESITY EPIDEMIC

Michaela Miller

**Consultant: Kathleen L. Keller, Ph.D.,
New York Obesity Research Center**

WORLD ALMANAC® LIBRARY

Please visit our web site at: www.garethstevens.com
For a free color catalog describing World Almanac® Library's list of
high-quality books and multimedia programs, call 1-800-848-2928 (USA)
or 1-800-387-3178 (Canada). World Almanac® Library's fax: (414) 332-3567.

Library of Congress Cataloging-in-Publication Data

Miller, Michaela, 1961-
    The obesity epidemic / Michaela Miller.
      p. cm. – (What if we do nothing?)
    Includes bibliographical references and index.
    ISBN-13: 978-0-8368-7756-4 (lib. bdg.)
    ISBN-13: 978-0-8368-8156-1 (softcover)
    1. Obesity–Juvenile literature. I. Title.
RC628.M52   2007
362.196'398–dc22   2006030445

First published in 2007 by
World Almanac® Library
A Member of the WRC Media Family of Companies
330 West Olive Street, Suite 100
Milwaukee, WI 53212 USA

Copyright © 2007 by World Almanac® Library.

Produced by Arcturus Publishing Limited
Editor: Alex Woolf
Designer: Peta Morey
Picture researcher: Glass Onion Pictures

World Almanac® Library editorial direction: Valerie J. Weber
World Almanac® Library editor: Leifa Butrick
World Almanac® Library art direction: Tammy West
World Almanac® Library graphic design: Charlie Dahl
World Almanac® Library production: Jessica Yanke and Robert Kraus

Picture credits: CORBIS: 10 (Karen Kasmauski), 17 (Pat Doyle), 19 (Mark Peterson), 33 (Peter
Turnley), 34 (Anders Ryman), 42 (Don Mason), 45 (Mark Ralston/Reuters).Rex: 7 (David Lissy),
22 (John Powell), 39 (Sipa Press).Science Photo Library: 4 (Simon Fraser), 8 (Steve Gschmeissner),
13 (Marcelo Brodsky), 14 (Mark Clarke), 21 (BSIP VEM), 26 (David Munns), 29 (National Cancer
Institute), 37 (Peter Menzel).TopFoto: 25 (Bob Daemmrich/The Image Works), 31 (Ellen B. Senisi/
The Image Works), 40 (Michael J. Doolittle/The Image Works).

Printed in China

1 2 3 4 5 6 7 8 9 10 09 08 07 06

Contents

CHAPTER 1

What Is Obesity?

The year is 2020. Sophie has little energy. She is constantly thirsty and tired all the time. Walking up the stairs in her house is a struggle these days. Sophie is just fourteen years old and lives in England. She has diabetes, which started because she was overweight. Her doctor has told her she must take insulin, change her diet, and exercise more, but Sophie watches about eight hours of television every day, hates exercise, and cannot stop eating chocolate and potato chips.

Her mother is desperate. She knows Sophie could die because of the health problems caused by obesity. The family has little money, and they do not know how much longer they will be able to pay for insulin. So many obese diabetics are enrolled in the national health care system that the service is running out of money and will not pay for Sophie's treatment.

In 2020, one-third of the adults in Great Britain are obese. The health problems associated with diabetes—kidney failure, blindness, and loss of limbs caused by circulation problems—are increasing. Children now have a lower life expectancy than their parents.

Obesity: The Facts

Obesity is a medical disorder that describes people who have so much extra body fat that it affects their health and ability to live normally. Obesity causes many health problems, including heart disease, diabetes, and certain cancers.

To find out if an adult is obese, doctors and scientists use the body mass index (BMI). The BMI is a calculation that shows if someone is underweight, normal weight, overweight, or obese. The BMIs for overweight and obesity are defined by the World Health Organization. To calculate a BMI in pounds and inches, multiply the weight in pounds by 703.1, divide that product by

A doctor discusses the need to lose weight with an obese patient. The patient may suffer from several health problems if he does not reach his target weight.

height in inches, and then divide that result again by height in inches. To calculate using the metric system, divide a person's weight in kilograms by their height in meters squared (kg/m^2).

Adults with a BMI between 25 and 30 are said to be overweight, while those with a BMI of 30 or more are classified as obese. The BMI for a normal weight range falls between 18.5 and 24.9, while anyone with a BMI of less than 18.5 is underweight. Generally, a man who is 35 to 40 pounds (16-18 kg) overweight for his height and a woman who is 30 pounds (13 kg) overweight for her height would be obese.

For a person who weighs 140 pounds and is 5 feet, 5 inches tall, multiply

140 lbs. x 703.1 = 98,434

98,434 / 65 inches = 1514.37

1514.37/ 65 inches = 23.29

The BMI is 23.29.

This chart can be used to figure out an adult's body mass index. Find the intersection of weight and height. This gives the BMI.

Height (centimeters)

Weight (kg)	150	152.5	155	157.5	160	162.5	165	167.5	170	172.5	175	177.5	180	182.5	185	187.5	190	Weight (lbs)
45	20	19	18	18	17	17	16	16	15	15	14	14	14	13	13	12	12	100
47	21	20	19	19	18	17	17	16	16	16	15	15	14	14	13	13	13	105
50	22	21	20	19	19	18	18	17	17	16	16	15	15	15	14	14	13	110
52	23	22	21	20	20	19	19	18	17	17	17	16	16	15	15	14	14	115
54	23	23	22	21	21	20	19	19	18	18	17	17	16	16	15	15	15	120
57	24	24	23	22	21	21	20	20	19	18	18	17	17	16	16	16	15	125
59	25	25	24	23	22	22	21	20	20	19	19	18	18	17	17	16	16	130
61	26	26	25	24	23	22	22	21	21	20	19	19	18	18	17	17	16	135
63	27	26	26	25	24	23	23	22	21	21	20	20	19	18	18	17	17	140
66	28	27	27	26	25	24	23	23	22	21	21	20	20	19	19	18	18	145
68	29	28	27	27	26	25	24	23	23	22	22	21	20	20	19	19	18	150
70	30	29	28	27	27	26	25	24	24	23	22	22	21	20	20	19	19	155
72	31	30	29	28	27	27	26	25	24	24	23	22	22	21	21	20	19	160
75	32	31	30	29	28	27	27	26	25	24	24	23	22	22	21	21	20	165
77	33	32	31	30	29	28	27	27	26	25	24	24	23	22	22	21	21	170
79	34	33	32	31	30	29	28	27	27	26	25	24	24	23	22	22	21	175
82	35	34	33	32	31	30	29	28	27	27	26	25	24	24	23	22	22	180
84	36	35	34	33	32	31	30	29	28	27	27	26	25	24	24	23	23	185
86	37	36	35	34	33	32	31	30	29	28	27	26	26	25	24	24	23	190
88	38	37	36	35	33	32	31	31	30	29	28	27	26	26	25	24	24	195
91	39	38	37	35	34	33	32	31	30	30	29	28	27	26	26	25	24	200
93	40	39	37	36	35	34	33	32	31	30	29	29	28	27	26	26	25	205
95	41	40	38	37	36	35	34	33	32	31	30	29	28	28	27	26	26	210
98	42	41	39	38	37	36	35	34	33	32	31	30	29	28	28	27	26	215
100	43	42	40	39	38	37	36	34	33	32	32	31	30	29	28	27	27	220
102	44	43	41	40	39	37	36	35	34	33	32	31	31	30	29	28	27	225
104	45	43	42	41	39	38	37	36	35	34	33	32	31	30	30	29	28	230
107	46	44	43	42	40	39	38	37	36	35	34	33	32	31	30	29	29	235
109	47	45	44	43	41	40	39	38	36	35	34	33	33	32	31	30	29	240
111	48	46	45	43	42	41	40	38	37	36	35	34	33	32	31	31	30	245
114	49	47	46	44	43	42	40	39	38	37	36	35	34	33	32	31	30	250
	5'0"	5'1"	5'2"	5'3"	5'4"	5'5"	5'6"	5'7"	5'8"	5'9"	5'10"	5'11"	6'0"	6'1"	6'2"	6'3"	6'4"	

Weight (kilograms) ... Weight (pounds)

Height (feet and inches)

Source: *Obesity: Third Report of Session* 2003-04 by the House of Commons Health Committee, 2004, page 131

Key   Underweight   Normal weight   Overweight   Obese

5

World Health Organization guidelines also use waist measurements to show if someone is obese. A man with a waist measurement of more than 40 inches (101.6 centimeters) and a woman with a waist measurement of more than 35 inches (89 cm) can be considered obese. This is called the waist circumference measurement.

Researchers have found that health problems caused by obesity can occur at different BMIs for people of different ethnic origin. For example, an overweight Asian man with a BMI of 27.5 or more is likely to have as many health problems and as great an increased risk of death as a Caucasian man with a BMI of 30.

Energy In, Energy Out

How do we gain extra weight? One of the simplest explanations is to look at the energy we put into our bodies and the energy that we use up through different activities. The body needs energy to work effectively, and it gets its energy from food. An active person will use up more energy than someone who is inactive.

The energy within food that we use up in our everyday lives is normally measured in kilojoules and kilocalories (calories for short). One kilojoule equals 1,000 joules of energy, and one calorie equals 4.1868 joules. The calorie is the most commonly used unit of measurement when referring to the energy values of food and the energy used up doing various activities.

COUNTING CALORIES

Different types of food contain different amounts of calories. For example, an average-sized apple contains about 53 calories, a chocolate bar may contain about 290 calories, and half a pound (.23 kg) of grilled chicken breast without the skin contains around 263 calories. Oil, butter, sauces—anything we might put on our food or that we use to cook it—contain calories, too. Chocolate bars, cakes, and cookies that contain a lot of fats and sugars contain more calories than the same amount of vegetables, fruits, or grilled meat.

To stay the same weight, a normally active man of average height, weighing 163 pounds (74 kg), and between nineteen and fifty years old, needs to take in about 2,550 calories a day. A normally active woman of average height, weighing 141 pounds (64 kg), and between nineteen and fifty, needs 1,940 calories. If people take in more calories than they use up, the unused energy is stored in their bodies as fat. Taller people usually need to take in more energy than shorter ones.

Active people like this runner use up more calories than people who are inactive. If someone takes in more calories than they actually use, they will gain weight.

Burning Energy

Different types of activities burn off different amounts of calories. To burn off the 294 calories contained in a chocolate bar, an average-sized, twenty-five-year-old man would have to walk moderately quickly for 59 minutes. To burn off the chocolate bar more quickly, the man could play tennis, jog, or dig for 47 minutes. The fastest way to burn off the calories in the chocolate bar would be to play football or swim freestyle for 39 minutes.

A Matter of Fat

When calories are not burned off, they are stored in the body as fat. It takes 3,500 unused calories to create 1 pound (.45 kg) of body fat. This fat can be burned off if a person becomes more active and uses more energy. If it is never burned off and more fat is stored, however, the BMI rises, and the person becomes overweight and eventually obese.

Fat is stored in cells that stop being created in the body at the end of puberty. Fat cells get bigger or smaller depending on the amount of fat stored within them. Because children who are overweight or at risk for overweight may have up to three times more fat cells in their bodies than children of normal weight, it is harder for them to lose weight. Even when they are adults, they will still have the same number of fat cells within their bodies. They will never be able to get rid of the actual cells, only the fat within them.

Fat Storage

Most fat is stored under the skin, but men and women store fat in different areas. Adult men tend to store fat around their chests, waists, and buttocks, giving them an apple shape when they are overweight or obese. Adult females usually store fat around their breasts, waists, hips, and chests, producing more of a pear shape. In both men and women, some fat is stored around the kidneys and inside the liver and muscles.

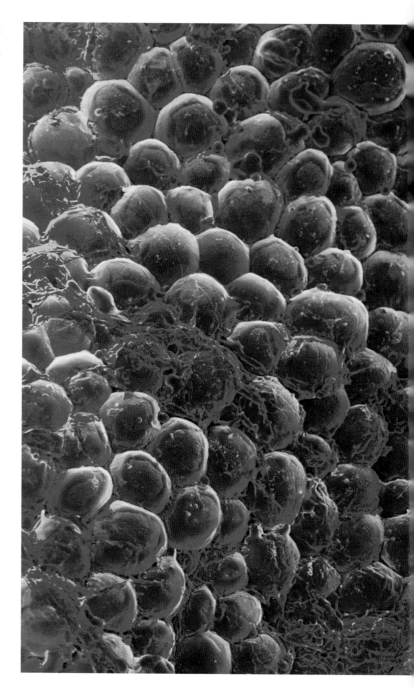

This image from a powerful microscope shows fat cells that are stored under the skin. Fat cells get bigger or smaller depending on the amount of fat within them.

Not all fat is bad. It is very important for humans to have some fat; otherwise, their bodies will not work properly.

A Worldwide Problem

Obesity is increasing all around the globe. The World Health Organization estimated that in 1995, 200 million people in the world were obese. By 2002, the number had risen to 300 million.

Obesity is traditionally associated with the richer countries in the developed world. In the United States, approximately 130 million adults are overweight or obese, and in Britain one-fifth of all adults are obese. In most European countries, the incidence of obesity has increased by between 10 and 40 percent over the past ten years.

This chart shows the percentage of men (right side of the bar) and women (left side) who are overweight or obese in twenty-nine countries.

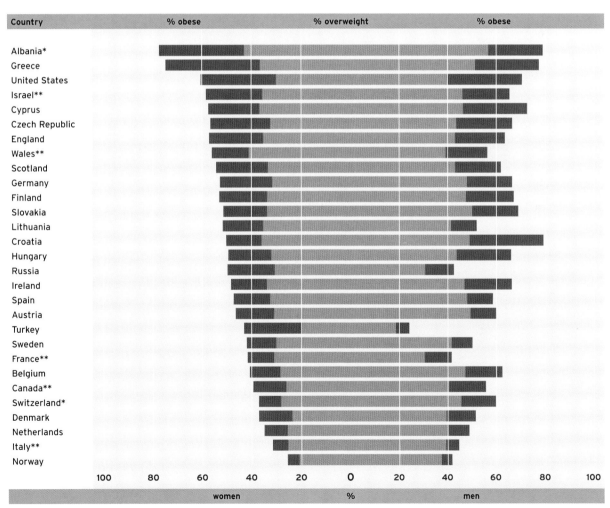

Source: International Obesity Task Force

* Urban ** Self-reported

Australia, a country traditionally associated with sports and the outdoor life, is also suffering from an obesity epidemic. Seven million Australians are already overweight or obese, and experts predict that 75 percent of the population will be overweight or obese by 2020.

Many parts of the developing world are now affected by the obesity crisis, too. In Africa, obesity has increased among those who have moved to the cities, while those in rural areas continue to go hungry. Ghana, for example, now has as many overweight as underweight people.

Increasing numbers of young people are overweight or at risk for overweight. These girls are at a special camp in the United States that tries to help them deal with their weight problems.

WHAT WOULD YOU DO?

You Are in Charge

Your country is facing an obesity crisis. Half the adult population is now obese, and their obesity-linked illnesses are putting a great strain on the national health care system. You are the government official responsible for public health and have the following choices:

- Do nothing about obesity because it is not the government's responsibility to tell people how to live.
- Conduct a national obesity awareness and healthy-eating campaign to inform people about the problem.
- Place a tax on foods that cause obesity to discourage people from buying them.

What would you do? See the discussion on page 47 for more suggestions.

CHAPTER 2

What Causes Obesity?

It is 2020 and a Saturday night in El Paso, Texas. Carlos and his family sit down in front of television, ready for their evening meal. Their favorite fast-food restaurant has just delivered four "two-for-the-price-of-one" king-sized meals. The family ordered them online, using the computer in the television set, without even leaving their chairs.

Most of the family's shopping is done this way. In 2020, people do not need to go to a restaurant to pick up take-out meals unless they want to. They also do not need to go to a supermarket and walk around. They can order online and get someone else to do their shopping for them.

In the old days, people used to walk or ride their bikes into the center of El Paso. Today, however, the downtown district has virtually closed down because many shopping malls are now on the outskirts of the city.

The number of cars on the roads makes it unsafe to ride bicycles. Children are not allowed to have bikes because riding them is too dangerous. Carlos looks forward to getting his driver's licence. In 2020, more than half the population in the United States is obese.

A Supersized Issue

Although the reasons for gaining weight seem obvious—a matter of taking in more energy than is actually used up—the actual causes of obesity are more complex. Food producers, advertising agencies, local and national governments, as well as the general public have all played a part in the current obesity crisis.

Too Much Food

In the 1970s, the population in Western nations was growing more slowly than the food supply. Instead of producing less food to match the needs of a smaller population, however, farmers, ranchers, canning companies, and dairy producers continued to grow and make more than was needed. People involved in the food industry, in that case, did not lose money or jobs.

But what happened to the extra food? One solution was to make people want to buy and eat more. New, supersized portions and low prices—particularly in the United States—encouraged people to overeat.

Food is now usually available twenty-four hours a day in the developed world. Supermarkets, fast-food restaurants, and street vendors are ready to sell whatever people want. The way we eat has also changed. It is acceptable to eat anywhere—on the way to school or work and on the way home after an evening out.

Here is a list of well-known foods, their calorie content, and the amount of activity required to burn off the calories.

| Food | Nutritional content | | Minutes required to burn off by activity | | |
	Calories	Fat grams	Walking slowly	Walking quickly	Strenuous activity
Mars Bar (2.3 ounces–65 grams)	294	11.4 (17%)	98	59	39
Popcorn (3.5 oz.–100g)	405	7.7 (7%)	135	81	54
Big Mac (8 oz.–215g)	492	23 (10.7%)	164	98	66
Cheeseburger (6 oz.–162g)	379	18.9 (11.6%)	126	76	51
Kentucky Fried Chicken (2.4 oz–67g)	195	12 (18 %)	65	39	26
Hamburger (4 oz.–108g)	254	7.7 (7%)	85	51	34
Pizza Deluxe (1 slice/2.3 oz.–66g)	171	6.7 (10%)	57	34	23
Pizza (4.75 oz.–135g)	263	4.9 (3.6%)	88	53	35
Potato Wedges (4.75 oz.–135g)	279	13 (10%)	93	56	37
Chicken Curry (5.25 oz–150g)	232	6.2 (4%)	77	46	31
Can of Coke (12 oz.–355 milliliters)	139	0 (0%)	46	28	19

Source: Obesity: Third Report of Session 2003-04 by the House of Commons Health Committee, 2004, page 134

Modern Life

People used to prepare meals three times a day and eat at home. In the home, the cook had complete control over the amount of fat and sugar that went into meals. This control is no longer possible when people buy restaurant food or ready-made meals from supermarkets.

In modern homes, food is always available. Large appliances like refrigerators and freezers allow us to buy and store plenty of food; microwaves allow us to cook it quickly. It has been a long time since someone would walk to the market, buy just enough food for a day or so, and carry it home.

The type of food that is available has also changed. Government policies like the European Union Common Agricultural Policy

(CAP) allow governments to pay farmers subsidies that reward farmers more for producing sugar and dairy products than for growing more fruit and vegetables.

Under the European Union Common Agricultural Policy, farmers are paid to produce extra sugar and dairy products. They are also paid to destroy any extra fruit and vegetables they grow rather than selling them more cheaply or even giving them away to people who cannot afford them. The result is that food that is high in fat and sugar is cheaper to buy than healthy options.

Nowadays, people rarely eat three meals a day in their homes. Food is available to take out and eat just about anywhere.

JUNK FOOD CONSUMED BY EACH AMERICAN YEARLY

- 50 pounds (22.7 kg) of cookies and cakes
- 100 pounds (45.4 kg) of refined sugar
- 55 pounds (25 kg) of fat and oil
- 300 cans of soft drink
- 200 sticks of chewing gum
- 20 gallons (75 liters) of ice cream
- 5 pounds (2.27 kg) of potato chips
- 18 pounds (8kg) of candy
- 2 pounds (.9 kg) of popcorn
- Unknown quantity of pretzels and other snack foods

Source: Elkort, Martin. The Secret Life of Food, 1991, p.125.

Snack or Meal?

Chocolate bars and bags of chips are thought of as snack foods—something to keep us going between meals if we get hungry. King-sized chocolate bars, however, weighing 3.5 ounces (100 grams) can contain as many as 400 calories. This is as many calories as a meal of lean grilled meat, potatoes, and green vegetables weighing 14 ounces (400 grams).

A chocolate bar is *energy dense*. It does not weigh very much, but it contains a lot of calories. Because the bar weighs very little compared to a meal, it does not create a lasting feeling of fullness, so the body feels it needs to eat something else soon.

Frequent snacking easily leads to quick weight gain. Eating one chocolate bar, a bag of potato chips, and one soft drink per day can put someone nearly 800 calories over the recommended adult intake. Just 400 unused calories a day, stored every day for a year, can result in a weight gain of 41 pounds (18.6 kg)!

The Power of Advertising

Advertising on television, at movie theaters, on the Internet, and in magazines may also be responsible for increasing obesity. Some countries, like Sweden, believe so strongly that advertising influences children that they have banned advertising from television during children's programs. Companies producing snack foods spend large sums of money advertising their products. In the United States, about $25 billion is spent annually on food and drink advertising. In 2002, $340 million was spent in Britain by companies advertising chocolate, sweets, and chips, whereas only $5.3 million was spent advertising fresh fruit. Most of the advertising focuses upon packaged and processed food.

Unhealthy foods like ice cream and chocolate are advertised and available just about everywhere. Manufacturers spend millions of dollars promoting junk food.

In contrast, government-backed healthy eating campaigns usually have much smaller advertising budgets. For example, in 1997, the Department of Agriculture spent $333 million on nutrition education, evaluation, and demonstrations—a relatively small amount in comparison with the billions spent by companies on food and drink advertising. The British government's healthy eating Five A Day campaign, promoting the need to eat five portions of fruit and vegetables every day to stay healthy, involved a relatively small advertising budget of $9.5 million in 2002.

Food companies promote their products in other ways, too. Cereal companies encourage people to collect proof of purchase seals to send in and redeem for toys. Sometimes a toy is inside a package to encourage people to buy the fattening treat.

Fast-food promotions that offer collectible toys to children as part of a meal may also contribute to the obesity problem. According to a British government report, one fast-food chain offered ninety-eight toys to collect in a year. To collect every toy, a child would have had to eat one high-calorie, high-fat fast-food meal every 3.7 days. A standard-sized children's meal from a fast-food restaurant containing one hamburger, an order of French fries, and a soft drink contains about 600 calories and .7 ounces (20 grams) of fat. The recommended intake for a normally active ten-year-old child is between 1,740 and 1,970 calories a day and 1.23 ounces (35 grams) of fat.

U.S. FOOD MARKETING AND ADVERTISING COST, 1997-1998

Breakfast cereals	$792 million
Candies and chocolate	$765 million
Soft drinks	$549 million
Snacks	$330 million

One fast-food hamburger chain spent $571 million advertising its products from 1997 to-1998.

Source: http://youthxchange.e-meta.net/main/getyoursnack.asp

Sitting Ducks

Inactivity also contributes to obesity. When we are not active, we burn off calories much more slowly—and modern life has made us more inactive than ever before. Watching television, which burns off very few calories, has had a big effect on our activity levels. In the average U.S. household, television watching has increased from five hours and seven minutes per day in 1960 to eight hours per day in 2003.

Computer games have also affected activity levels. Children who are allowed to play them anytime and for as long as they want are less likely to run around and play outside.

People also walk less to get to any destination. In the United States, Americans go on foot for only 5.4 percent of their trips. They use cars to drive very short distances. The number of walks Americans take for distances of less than a mile (1.6 km) has decreased by 42 percent in twenty years. The average person in Britain now walks 189 miles (304.2 kilometers) per year—66 miles (106.2 km) less than twenty-five years ago.

New Zealand, traditionally associated with outdoor sports and walking, has noticed a similar decline. Trips made on foot dropped 3 percent to 400,000 a day between 1989 and 1998; one-third of the automobile trips were for distances of less than 1.24 miles (2 km).

WHAT WOULD YOU DO?

You Are in Charge
As the head of a company that makes potato chips, you have been accused of encouraging obesity with your products. You are worried that customers might stop buying your chips if they think the chips will make them fat. You want to find some way to keep your customers happy and keep people from becoming overweight.

What would you do?

Bicycling used to be a popular way of getting around, but people are bicycling less and less, mostly because of safety concerns. There are few bicycle lanes and more cars. In Britain in 1952, people bicycled 14.3 billion miles (23 billion km), but now people only ride 2.48 billion miles (4 billion km). The sight of children riding bikes, playing outside, and walking to school is also not as common as it used to be because parents are concerned about safety.

Children who watch lots of television are less likely to play active games outdoors, and they will gain weight because of their inactivity.

Other Causes

Hereditary factors help to explain why some people gain weight more easily than others. Researchers have found that some families have slower metabolisms than others. Their bodies burn up energy more slowly, which means they are more inclined to gain weight than families with faster metabolisms.

Psychological factors also make people overeat. Some people overeat because they are unhappy, bored, or depressed. Food represents a form of comfort to them.

Obesity and Health

Peter's father is a doctor at a hospital in Munich, Germany. He arrives home from work and tells his family in despair, "Today we had such bad news. We cannot afford any more kidney dialysis machines for the hospital. Our waiting lists are very long, and I know that people—some of them children—are going to die before we can treat them. How can I face their parents? How can I do my job properly?"

It is May 2020. Peter is twelve years old. He is one of the lucky ones. His parents were determined that he would not become part of the obesity crisis they heard about at the beginning of the century. Peter's diet has been healthy, and the family makes sure he gets the recommended hour of exercise every day. Peter's family is rare, however. In his town, more than 30 percent of the children under twelve are obese diabetics. Some of them are in such poor condition that they need dialysis—a treatment to rid the blood of toxins. When kidneys fail, patients need treatment within three months, or they will die.

Health Problems

Obesity increases the chances of people suffering from serious and even fatal diseases, such as heart disease, type 2 diabetes, and different types of cancer. Because of these and other health problems, someone who is obese will probably live nine years less than a person of normal weight.

What is Diabetes?

Diabetes develops when the body cannot use glucose (sugar) properly. This condition occurs when there is not enough of the hormone insulin in the body or when the insulin available simply does not work properly. Insulin is made and stored in an organ called the pancreas.

There are two types of diabetes—type 1 and type 2. In type 1 diabetes, the body is unable to produce any insulin. This type of diabetes usually starts in childhood or young adulthood. These diabetics must change their diet and inject themselves with insulin. Type 1 diabetes used to be called insulin-dependent diabetes or juvenile diabetes.

In type 2 diabetes, the pancreas may not produce enough insulin, or its insulin does not work properly. This condition affects people as they get older and usually appears after the age of forty. It used to be known as maturity-onset diabetes or non-insulin-dependent diabetes.

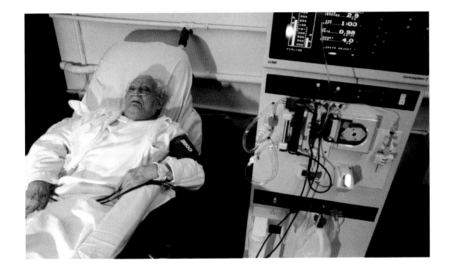

A patient undergoing kidney dialysis. Obesity can cause type 2 diabetes, which may lead to kidney failure. Dialysis is then needed to do the kidneys' job of eliminating toxins from the blood.

Type 2 diabetes is also associated with being overweight or obese. It is increasing among obese children and young adults. The American Diabetic Association has predicted that one in three American children born in 2000 will become diabetic at some time.

This chart shows how those with high body mass indexes are more likely to develop certain medical conditions.

Prevalence of Medical Conditions by Body Mass Index								
	Men Body Mass Index				Women Body Mass Index			
Medical Condition	8.5 to 24.9	25 to 29.9	30 to 34.9	over 40	8.5 to 24.9	25 to 29.9	30 to 34.9	over 40
Type 2 diabetes	2.03	4.93	10.1	10.65	2.38	7.12	7.24	19.89
Coronary heart disease	8.84	9.6	16.01	13.97	6.87	11.13	12.56	19.22
High blood pressure	23.47	34.16	48.95	64.53	23.26	38.77	47.95	63.16
Osteoarthritis	2.59	4.55	4.66	10.04	5.22	8.51	9.94	17.19

Prevalence ratio (%)

Source: American Obesity Association / NHANES III, 1988-1994

The Effects of Diabetes

Diabetes can be treated in several ways. People who have it may receive insulin injections or pills, go on special diets, or combine any of these treatments.

If diabetes is not treated, it can cause heart disease, stroke, blindness, and kidney failure. Diabetes can also damage the nerves, making people less aware of pressure or injury to parts of their bodies. Some people develop large sores on their feet or legs as a result, and sometimes doctors have to amputate a patient's limbs.

One of the worst effects of diabetes is what it does to the kidneys' ability to do their job. Over time, the high levels of sugar in the blood damages the millions of tiny filtering units within each kidney.

The kidneys' function is to cleanse the blood of toxins and transform waste in the body into urine. The body's two kidneys can get rid of about 3 quarts (2.74 liters) of urine per day. When they do not work properly, harmful salts and fluids build up in the body, and then dialysis—removing the toxins from the blood with a machine—may be necessary.

In the United States, kidney dialysis and kidney transplants cost more than $35 billion annually. Treatment for kidney failure currently costs Britain's National Health Service $3.8 billion each year, and the figure is growing.

Heart Problems

People who are overweight or obese need more oxygen, and so their bodies have to create more blood. The heart then has to work harder pumping this blood through the body. This work, in turn, puts such

CANCER

Certain types of cancer are linked with obesity. In men and women, obesity is associated with cancers of the esophagus, colon, rectum, liver, gall bladder, pancreas, and kidneys. Obese women may also suffer from cancers of the breast, uterus, and cervix. Obese men have a higher chance of getting stomach and prostate cancer.

a strain on the heart that it can damage it and cause high blood pressure.

Obesity is also linked with heart disease. One form of heart disease is atherosclerosis—a buildup of fat within the walls of the arteries. This fat narrows the arteries and reduces the space through which blood can flow. These materials may also block the delivery of nutrients to the artery walls, making them less strong and healthy. Extra fat will make it harder for the blood to move through the veins and carry the oxygen that the body needs to survive. Heart disease also means that the blood is more inclined to clot, which can lead to a life-threatening condition called thrombosis and make heart attacks more likely.

People with heart disease can experience a feeling of heaviness, tightness, or pain in the middle of their chest that affects the rest of their upper body, too. Running, playing sports, or even going upstairs can bring on the symptoms. They may feel constantly tired.

This highly magnified artery is clogged with fat. Heart disease is a buildup of fat within the arteries, which makes it more difficult for blood to move through the body.

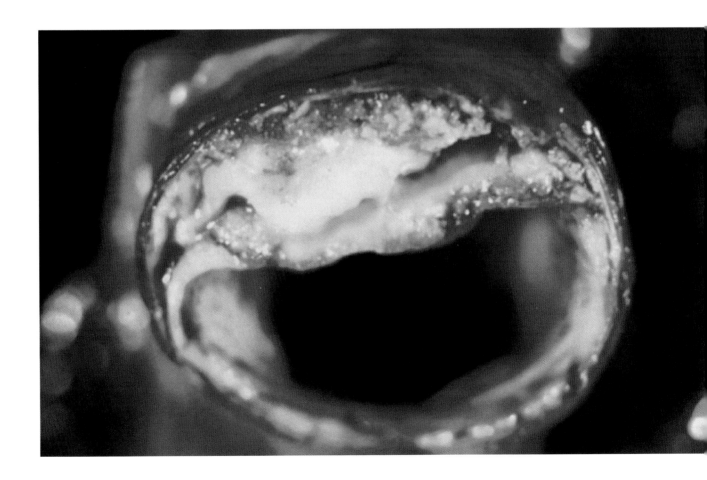

Heart disease can be treated by drugs. If arteries are badly blocked, drugs may not work, and the patient may need surgery to open up or replace the arteries.

Osteoarthritis

Extra weight places an increased strain on the body's joints, and this, in turn, can lead to osteoarthritis, a disease affecting the joints. This disorder can become very disabling and painful.

Psychological Problems

Sadly, obese people are often depressed because they feel bad about themselves and are sometimes treated badly by others. Obese women are 37 percent more likely to commit suicide than women of a healthy weight.

Counting the Cost

The health problems caused by obesity affect people's ability to do their jobs. In the United States, for example, 130 million adults are overweight or obese, and this costs an estimated $117 billion in medical expenses and lost productivity. Severely obese Americans are 60 percent more expensive to treat than Americans of normal weight.

Obesity can make people feel very bad about themselves; they may even suffer from depression.

Obesity costs Britain's National Health Service $950 million per year in terms of treatment. The wider cost to industry in terms of lost working days brings the total cost to more than $3.8 billion. The Australian government estimates that obesity costs its country $1.5 billion per year in direct health costs.

If obesity continues to rise among young people, medical and economic costs will also continue to grow. The rising costs may lead to the need for tax increases in countries with a government-funded health-care service. In countries without a national health-care service, medical costs will rise, and obese people will risk becoming impoverished and even dying because they cannot afford treatment.

Estimates of the Direct Costs of Obesity			Prevalance of Obesity (BMI over 30)	
Country	Year of estimate	Proportion of total health-care expenditure due to obesity	At time of estimate (%)	2003 (%)
United States	2000	4.8	30.5	30.5
Netherlands	1981-89	4.0	5.0	10.3
Canada	1997	2.4	14.0	13.9
Portugal	1996	3.5	11.5	14.0
Australia	1989-90	more than 2.0	10.8	22.0
England	1998	1.5	19.0	23.5
France	1992	1.5	6.5	9.0

Source: Obesity: Third Report of Session 2003-04 by the House of Commons Health Committee, 2004, page 123

Treating Adult Obesity

Obese adults need medical treatment from specialists who can provide weight-loss programs, nutritional education, and counseling. Sometimes, it is helpful to use drugs to suppress appetites or drugs that can affect the way the body absorbs fat. Surgery may also reduce the stomach size of obese people so that they feel full after eating a small amount.

This table estimates how much money was spent on obesity-related illnesses in several countries compared to the total health care expenditure. It also shows how the obesity rate has changed in those countries since the estimates were made.

WHAT WOULD YOU DO?

You Are in Charge
You are a principal in a country where there is an obesity epidemic. The effects are obvious at your school. You are considering a ban on candy, potato chips, and other foods that are high in fat or sugar.

■ Could such a policy work?
■ What are the consequences?
■ What else could be done?

See the discussion on page 47.

CHAPTER 4

Obesity in Children and Young People

Alice is seventeen and president of a student council in New York State in 2020. She attends school board meetings and listens to the problems her school faces. The buildings need repair, but the district has no money for repairs. Education has received little government funding recently. People in the district cannot afford to pay more property tax because their health-care insurance payments—caused by the country's growing obesity crisis—are already too high.

More than half the students in Alice's school are overweight or at risk for being overweight. The school is in a poor part of town with few places for keeping fit. Even the local swimming pool is too expensive for most people. Many of the children in the area have joint problems because they are so heavy, and they find it hard to walk even short distances without getting out of breath.

Today, Alice, the school board, and the principal must decide whether to accept an offer to sell the last school athletics field to a developer who wants to build a shopping mall. The money can be used to repair the school buildings, but school is the only place that some children get any exercise at all. The health of the students will suffer without this athletics field.

A Growing Problem

Although most overweight children or children at risk of being overweight do not have serious health problems while they are young, they are very likely to suffer health problems if they remain overweight or become obese as they grow up. Researchers have found that overweight young people have a greater chance of being overweight adults, and that weight problems seem to run in families. The American Obesity Association reports that overweight children age ten to fourteen who have at least one overweight or obese parent have a 79 percent chance of being overweight adults.

Like adults, young people gain weight if they eat more than they burn off. Unused energy becomes fat cells, which the body produces until the end of puberty.

Poor eating habits, lack of activity, and the resulting weight gain can affect whole families.

DEFINING CHILDHOOD OBESITY

Definitions of childhood obesity vary from country to country, but the 1998 guidelines from the Centers for Disease Control (CDC) state that the word *obese* should not be used for children at all because the word does not take children's growth spurts and sex differences into account. The organization also recommends not using the term because it could be psychologically harmful. Instead, it uses the terms *at risk for overweight* and *overweight*. The organization compares the weight of today's children to growth charts of children's weight during the 1960s and 1970s when fewer children were overweight. Children at risk for being overweight have BMIs higher than 85 to 94 percent of all children their age during the 1960 and 1970s. Overweight children have BMIs higher than 95 percent of all children their age during the same time period.

Fat Programming

During puberty, sex hormones—estrogen for girls, and testosterone for boys—begin to increase. These hormones define where fat cells grow. Once fat cells are established, when puberty ends, these cells can get bigger or smaller depending on the amount of fat in them. There is nothing anyone can do to get rid of fat cells. People can only burn up fat within the cells.

Because they have many fat cells within their bodies, people who were overweight as children have trouble losing weight when they are older. Their bodies seem naturally overweight. Children who are at risk of being overweight or overweight sometimes have up to three times as many fat cells in their bodies as children of normal weight.

The Scale of the Issue

Many doctors and scientists believe that overweight among children is a serious issue that is likely to get worse if no one does anything. The World Health Organization (WHO) has estimated that 3.3 percent of the world's preschool children are now

A food pyramid shows the recommended amount of different types of food needed for a healthy diet.

Grains	Vegetables	Fruits	Milk	Meat & Beans
Make half your grains whole	Vary your veggies	Focus on fruits	Get your calcium-rich foods	Go lean with protein

Oils — Oils are not a food group, but you need some for good health. Get your oils from fish, nuts, and liquid oils such as corn oil, soybean oil, and canola oil.

overweight. The number of overweight children in Britain has tripled in twenty years. Ten percent of six-year-olds are overweight and 17 percent of fifteen-year-olds. In the United States, 30.3 percent of children age six to eleven are at risk of being overweight and 15 percent are overweight. About 30.3 percent of U.S. adolescents age twelve to nineteen are at risk of being overweight, and 15 percent are overweight.

Treating Obesity in Children

In adults, the body mass index (BMI) is used as an indicator of obesity. The BMI is also applied in the case of children, but it is used alongside other growth charts that take into account children's rate of growth, their height, their sex, and their age.

Many experts believe that it is not a good idea for children who are at risk for being overweight to go on a diet because this could affect their growth. Placing such children on strict diets can also make them feel bad about themselves. Low self-esteem can lead to anorexia nervosa, a psychological illness that makes people eat increasingly less until they severely damage their health and sometimes even die.

Children at risk for overweight are usually encouraged to maintain their weight—not gain any more. Doctors expect that as these children grow, their weight will more closely align with their

Age	Males (calories)	Females (calories)
0–3 months	545	515
4–6 months	690	645
7–9 months	825	765
10–12 months	920	865
1–3 years	1,230	1,165
4–6 years	1,715	1,545
7–10 years	1,970	1,740
11–14 years	2,220	1,845
15–18 years	2,755	2,110
19–50 years	2,550	1,940
51–59 years	2,550	1,900
60–64 years	2,380	1,900
65–74 years	2,330	1,900
over 74 years	2,100	1,810

This chart shows the average estimated calorie requirements for people of different ages.

Source: Obesity: Third Report of Session 2003-04 by the House of Commons Health Committee, 2004, page 132

height. They are also advised to take part in more physical activity. Walking, swimming, cycling, aerobics, and other sports can all help to stop further weight gain. British and American government guidelines state that children need at least one hour of physical activity per day to stay healthy. The most effective prescription for children at risk of being overweight is to change their eating habits by cutting out junk foods, adopting a healthy, well-balanced diet, and exercising more.

Children who are already overweight face more serious challenges. Usually they need help from doctors, dietitians, and counselors, and so do their families. Overweight children may be given counseling about the kind of foods that are good for them and put on a diet. In some countries, extremely overweight children may have an operation to reduce the size of their stomachs so that they feel full after eating a small amount of food. Although drugs are available to treat adult obesity, none of them is recommended for children under sixteen.

The Causes of Obesity in Children

Many factors contribute to obesity in young people.

Genetic Inheritance: Scientists have found some evidence that, in a small number of cases, obesity can be inherited. Researchers have identified families that have low metabolic rates. A slow metabolism means that the body does not burn off calories very quickly so it is easier to gain weight.

Scientists have also found that some genes can increase or decrease appetites. Some people, therefore, feel more hungry than others or have to eat a lot before they feel full. As a result, these people have a tendency to overeat and gain weight. Further, there is some evidence that genes can influence food preferences. These genes may determine whether people naturally choose to eat sweet or spicy foods.

Period	Percentage of US children (age 6 to 11) who are overweight		Percentage of US adolescents (age 12 to 19) who are overweight	
	Boys	Girls	Boys	Girls
1971-1974	4.3	3.6	6.1	6.2
1988-1994	11.6	11	11.3	9.7
1999-2000	16	14.5	15.5	15.5

This chart shows how obesity has increased among U.S. children since 1974.

Source: Obesity: CDC, National Center for Health Statistics, National Health and Nutrition Examination Survey. Ogden et al. JAMA. 2002;288:1728-1732.

Birth Weight: Studies have suggested that people are more likely to become obese later in life if they had low birth weights because they did not get the nourishment they needed when they were developing in the womb. The evidence for this is much stronger than evidence linking high birth weights to obesity in later life.

Breast Feeding: Research has also shown that breast-fed babies may be less at risk of becoming overweight. A team at the Cincinnati Children's Hospital Medical Center found high levels of a protein that affects the body's processing of fat in breast milk. In Scotland, scientists studied thirty-two thousand children and found 30 percent fewer overweight children among those who had been breast fed as babies. Many scientists believe that feeding babies breast milk for the first six to twelve months of their lives is the best way to prevent obesity in children.

This shopping cart is full of unhealthy, highly processed food. Most experts say that a healthy diet should include at least five portions of fruit and vegetables per day.

Overeating: Children who eat more calories than they burn off are likely to become overweight. High-fat foods and foods that are mostly sugar contain more calories and are, as a result, harder to burn off. Processed foods are more likely to contain hidden fats than similar items made at home.

Inactivity: If people are inactive, the calories they eat will not be burned off. Children who do not take part in physical activities and who prefer to watch television or play computer games are more likely to gain weight. Some research has linked obesity directly with television viewing, reporting that the more television people watch, the fatter they become.

Social and Economic Factors: Some research shows that people in deprived areas who have not had a good education are more likely to become obese. High-fat, high-sugar foods like potato chips and cakes are cheaper for many families than healthy alternatives like fresh fruit and vegetables.

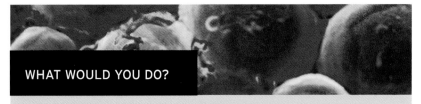

WHAT WOULD YOU DO?

You Are in Charge
You are a parent. How would you encourage your over-weight children to watch less television, exercise more, and eat properly? What do you believe other people could do to help fight childhood obesity?

■ The government?
■ Food producers?
■ Advertising agencies?

Should advertisements for unhealthy foods be banned? What would you do?

Effects on Health

Being overweight in childhood can lead to various health problems, including the development of type 2 diabetes. High blood pressure is nine times more common in overweight children than in children whose weight is normal. Overweight children can also suffer from orthopedic complaints such as bowing of the leg bones.

Some obese children and adults suffer from snoring and sleep apnea, disordered breathing, as they try to sleep. Too much fat in the chest wall and abdomen makes it hard to breathe normally, and the capacity of the lungs is actually reduced. Fat also collects around the upper airway, particularly the larynx, which may stop the air going through these passages at night when someone is lying down.

Psychological Problems

Sadly, children who are overweight or at risk for being overweight can also suffer psychological problems because of their size. Many report that they are teased and bullied about their weight at school and that friends, family, and even strangers make hurtful comments. The effects of name-calling can last a long time.

As a result, it is quite common for overweight young people to feel very bad about themselves. Some suffer from depression. Some may not go out at all to avoid being bullied. As they grow heavier, they may not want to change clothes in front of others. This often keeps them from going swimming or attending gym classes that provide the exercise they need to burn up extra fat.

Sometimes overweight children are bullied in school. This can damage their self-esteem and make them eat even more to try to make themselves feel better.

CHAPTER 5

Obesity in the Developing World

Sanjeev takes off his school uniform for the last time. He is thirteen years old, and tomorrow he starts work breaking up stones in the local quarry. There, with his three brothers, he will work from dawn to dusk for just a few rupees a day.

Once, Sanjeev thought he would be a doctor, but this is no longer possible. His family no longer has any money to send him to school. All his brothers and sisters need to work now to keep their father alive.

Sanjeev's father was once a well-to-do manager of a computer call center. Like many people with well-paid jobs in India, however, he ate too much, gained too much weight, and then developed diabetes. He is now almost blind and too ill to work; he depends on his family to pay for the insulin injections that he needs several times a day.

The year is 2020, and families like this live in cities all over India. In the old days, people in India never seemed to have enough food to eat. In some rural areas, they still do not, but in the cities, many people are overweight or obese. There is not enough money to pay for their treatment. India now has the highest rate of diabetes in the world.

A Worldwide Epidemic

Obesity is usually thought of as a health issue that affects people who live in developed nations such as the United States and Britain. Recent research, however, shows that obesity is a problem that is spreading outside the West. The World Health Organization estimates that 300 million adults in the world are obese, and 115 million of them live in developing countries.

Not all developing countries keep statistics on obesity, but the statistics that are available show a growing problem that experts believe should be watched carefully. They are worried that the rising obesity rate could cause developing countries to go further into debt as they try to fight hunger on one hand and obesity on the other.

Africa, so often associated with starvation and famine, now has many obese people in some areas. In Zambia, nearly 20 percent of the adults are obese, as are 25 percent of Egyptian adults.

In the Cape Peninsula of South Africa, 44 percent of the adult women suffer from obesity, while Ghana has as many overweight as underweight people. Most of the world's hungry people live in sub-Saharan Africa, and yet more and more educated women living in sub-Saharan cities are obese.

Although many people in Africa do not have enough food to eat, obesity is increasing in some African towns and cities.

DIABETES

One of the most serious obesity-related diseases in the developing world is diabetes. India, for example, now has the world's largest diabetic population, with more than 32 million people affected. About 85 percent of these have type 2 diabetes, and 90 percent of type 2 diabetics are obese or overweight. The number of diabetics in India is expected to more than double by 2025.

By that time, most people with diabetes in the developing world will be forty-five to sixty-four. Diabetes is the leading cause of blindness in people between twenty and seventy-four. A low-income Indian family with an adult with diabetes may have to spend 25 percent of the family income on diabetes care.

Samoan chiefs gather for a meeting. More than 79 percent of Samoan men living in urban areas are now obese.

FEAST OR FAMINE?

- More than 8 percent of North African children are at risk for being overweight, while 7 percent are starving.
- In eastern Asia, 4.3 percent of preschool children are at risk for being overweight, and 3.4 percent are starving.
- Some countries, including Egypt, Malawi, Nigeria, and Qatar, have a higher percentage of overweight children than the United States.

Other available statistics from around the developing world are equally upsetting: Thirty percent of Chile's adult population are obese; Thai children are showing a rise in obesity. In China, the number of overweight people increased from 10 to 15 percent in three years. In Brazil and Colombia, about 40 percent of the people are overweight; this number is similar to the percentage of people who are overweight in European countries.

An Urban Cause

This increase in obesity occurs mainly in the cities of developing countries. Many researchers believe that adopting Western lifestyles as people move from rural areas to the cities has been the cause of the increase.

Life in the rural areas of developing countries involves plenty of physical labor, including farming, collecting wood, carrying water, and walking from place to place. In the cities, however, more people own cars. People walk less and take either cars or buses to work. Many city dwellers work in offices, and they have a much less active lifestyle than people who live in rural areas.

This chart shows the percentage of women who are overweight in various parts of the developing world.

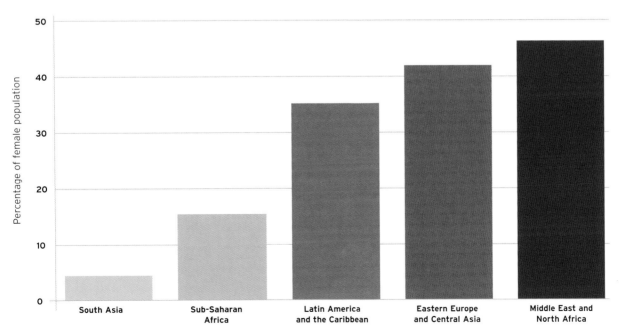

Source: R. Martorell, International Food Policy Research Institute, 2001.

The diet of people living in cities is different, too. A traditional African rural diet is based on roots, tubers, and coarse grains. In the cities, however, people eat Western-style, high-sugar, high-fat, processed foods and drinks. It is also easy to buy and eat food outside the home. Street vendors and food stalls are open seven days a week and until late at night, and food is almost always available, as it is in developed nations.

Although city dwellers are becoming heavier than their rural counterparts, they are also likely to suffer from malnutrition. They can suffer from iron deficiency and anemia as well as Vitamin A deficiency because large quantities of cheap food fill the stomach but may not give the body important vitamins and minerals.

The Effects of a Modern Lifestyle

The Pima Indians of Arizona are an example of a group of native people that has switched from a traditional diet to a Western, urban diet. The diet of most Arizona Pimas contains about 40 percent fat, and, on the average, they take part in physical activity for about two hours per week. In contrast, Pima Indians living in Mexico follow an active lifestyle that involves twenty-three hours of physical work per week and a traditional, low-fat diet. Arizona Pimas have a high incidence of obesity and type 2 diabetes compared with Mexican

This table shows how the effects of modernization—inactivity and a change of diet—can cause obesity in urban areas of developing countries.

Location or type of activity	Effect of modernization	Impact on obesity
Transportation	More people own cars. People walk or ride bikes less.	People get less exercise.
At home	More people use modern appliances (e.g., microwaves, dishwashers, washing machines, vacuum cleaners).	Housework burns up fewer calories.
	More ready-made foods and ingredients are available for cooking.	People eat more high-fat convenience foods that contribute to obesity.
	More people watch television and play computer and video games.	People spend less time on active recreational pursuits.
In the workplace	More people have desk jobs, which do not use up much energy, due to technology, especially increased computer use.	Work is less physically demanding.
Public places	More people use elevators, escalators, and automatic doors.	People get less exercise from climbing stairs and opening doors.
Living in the city	Increase in crime in urban areas.	Women, children, and the elderly go out alone less frequently for exercise and recreational activities.

Source: American Obesity Association

Pimas. Studies of the Pimas have helped scientists learn more about the causes and effects of obesity.

Counting the Cost

The governments of developing countries are currently fighting many health problems, including malnutrition and diseases such as typhoid, malaria, and cholera. The health problems associated with increasing obesity have the potential to create another burden on their already overstretched medical resources.

Nevertheless, despite the increase in obesity, hunger is still considered the biggest problem in the developing world. United Nations figures estimate that of the world's 815 million hungry people, 780 million live in developing countries.

A Pima Indian from Arizona is tested in water to determine his percentage of body fat.

WHAT WOULD YOU DO?

You Are in Charge

You are a government official in a developing country. What steps can you take to combat the growing problem of obesity in your country? How do the problems you face compare with those faced by governments in developed nations?

You are also one of the world's biggest producers of sugarcane. You would like to make sure that the sugarcane industry and its workers are on your side in the fight against obesity.

What would you do?

CHAPTER 6

Creating a Healthy Future

At the United Nations Youth Summit in 2020, young people from around the world exchange information on how the current obesity crisis affects their lives. Kyle, an eighteen-year-old American delegate, is angry. He blames governments, food producers, and retailers for encouraging a culture of overeating that is destroying the health of millions of people.

Kyle speaks from experience. His father died from heart disease last year, and the family is suing a fast-food chain, demanding money for his death. Kyle believes that his father's life was shortened by years of eating the chain's salty, high-fat food.

This legal action is like cases in the 1990s when families of smokers successfully sued tobacco companies for causing cancer in their loved ones. Kyle knows that the money will not bring his father back, but he wants to make the fast-food chain take responsibility and, at the same time, draw attention to millions of other families in similar situations all around the world.

Turning the Tide

Individuals cannot stop the obesity crisis by themselves. Obesity is a complex problem, and the solutions need action and commitment from people working together in many different areas. Governments, educators, health professionals, food producers, and retailers all need to cooperate to stop the rising tide of obesity. National and local governments have the power to create laws and pursue policies that can affect the health of a nation.

New laws could make it easier for people to get more exercise. For example, builders of roads, housing developments, shopping centers, and office buildings could be required to provide good sidewalks and safe bicycle lanes. New buildings could showcase beautiful staircases and make elevators and escalators more difficult

To try to stop the increase in obesity among their workers, some companies, like this one in Japan, have introduced fitness classes during working time.

to reach. Local governments could make sure that everyone has the opportunity to go to parks with exercise facilities and to inexpensive and accessible recreational centers.

Governments can also provide incentives to farmers to produce more fruit and vegetables. Currently, such incentives are rarely provided, and many policies seem to work against a nation's health. American agricultural policy, like the European Common Agricultural Policy (CAP), is an example of rewarding farmers for producing more food of one type than people need. Since the 1930s, American farmers have received subsidies to produce crops like wheat, soybeans, and corn. These subsidies were designed to keep American farmers at work and to provide enough food for the nation. Little financial incentive is offered to farmers to produce fruits, vegetables, and other grains.

This graph compares rates of coronary heart disease with fruit and vegetable consumption among men thirty-five to seventy-four, across eleven European countries. The graph shows that the higher the consumption of fruit and vegetables in a particular country, the lower the death rate from heart disease.

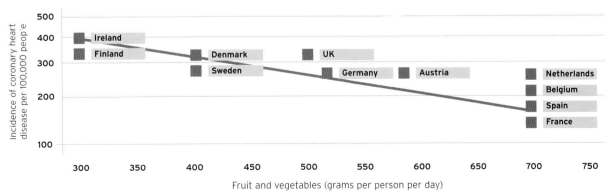

Source: Food and Agriculture Organization

Although corn may be a healthy vegetable, it is turned into a high-calorie, commonly used sweetener called high-fructose corn syrup (HFCS). Similarly, the oil from soybeans, which are nutritious, is used to make unhealthy foods such as salad dressing, cooking oil, margarine, and shortening. By switching subsidies from these crops to fruit and vegetables, governments could make a big difference in the battle against obesity.

Governments can also place restrictions on the promotion and advertising of unhealthy food. In some parts of the world, governments have banned advertising junk food to children on television. Norway has banned all television advertisements during the broadcast of children's programs, and the province of Quebec in Canada has banned advertising aimed at children under thirteen. Placing a tax on unhealthy food to discourage people from buying it —in much the same way as alcohol and cigarettes are taxed—is another option.

Education for Change

Education plays a vital role in encouraging children to lead healthier lifestyles. Obesity levels could be reduced by the introduction of healthy school meals, snack shops and vending machines that sell fruit, freely available drinking water, breakfast clubs, and a variety of fitness activities designed to appeal to all children.

School exercise and activity programs, such as this one in Schenectady, New York, are an important way of helping young people become fit and healthy.

Some countries have already taken steps in this direction. In Scotland, school vending machines must provide water and fruit juice, and advertisements on the machines promoting sugary drinks and unhealthy snacks are banned. England offers a National School Fruit Scheme, which offers every child from four to six years old a free piece of fruit each day.

Singapore introduced a ten-year Trim and Fit Scheme in 1992 that trained teachers in healthy eating and activities. The program also reduced sugar in children's drinks and increased physical activity for children during school hours. The program was successful in improving children's fitness and led to a reduction in the national level of childhood obesity.

SINGAPORE SUCCESS STORY

In 1992, Singapore government research found that 14 percent of the country's schoolchildren were overweight. The Trim and Fit Scheme was introduced to change this number. Under this program, children who were overweight or at risk of being overweight participated in 1.5 hours of exercise per week in addition to weekly physical education sessions. They also received nutritional counseling. Schools followed guidelines for the types of food that could be sold on the premises. By 2002, the percentage of children that were overweight was reduced to 9.8 percent.

Healthy Schools

Education about healthy lifestyles and how to choose and prepare healthy food could also be introduced into school curricula. Nutrition experts believe that the trend toward convenience foods—which simply have to be heated up and eaten—has meant that people have lost cooking skills.

Young people need to be empowered to make healthy choices in their lives. Lessons about citizenship and education about personal, social, and health choices, as well as school policies that encourage positive decision-making, can help empower young people.

By working closely with health-care centers, health professionals, and parents, schools can also provide support for young people who are overweight or at risk of being overweight. They can help them to change their eating habits and exercise more. Schools could also prevent overweight children or children at risk of being overweight from being bullied by their classmates.

Health Service in Crisis

If nothing is done to halt the current dramatic increase in obesity, health services throughout the world are likely to become severely overstretched. To prevent this from happening, doctors, nurses, and other health professionals need to be trained and given funding to

If food packages are labeled correctly, including the percentages of fat, sugar, and salt the food contains, it is easier for people to make healthy choices.

spread healthy eating and healthy lifestyle messages throughout their communities. Areas with high numbers of overweight and obese people would need extra help and funding.

Selling and Producing Food

Food retailers and supermarkets have an essential role to play in halting the obesity crisis. They can stock a wider range of healthy foods and offer them at prices that poorer customers can afford. They also can encourage shoppers to buy them through healthy eating campaigns. By removing sweets and salty snack foods from the checkout areas, supermarkets can reduce their customers' exposure to unhealthy choices.

The battle against obesity can also be helped by clearer and more accurate food labeling. People frequently do not appreciate what is in the food they buy because the labels are not easily understood. Laws could ensure that labels present the product's nutritional content in a way that is easily understood and not misleading. For example, the phrase "85 percent fat free" does not clearly say that the product actually contains 15 percent fat. Similarly, a product that is labeled "fat free" could still be high in sugar.

North Karelia Project

An example of how a government can work with health professionals, teachers, food producers, and retailers to improve the

This chart shows the improvements in the coronary heart disease mortality rate among men aged thirty-five to sixty-four in North Karelia and Finland as a result of the North Karelia project.

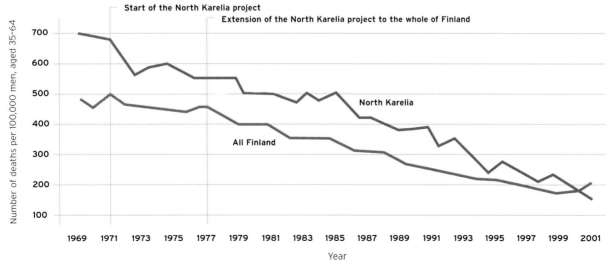

Source: Heart views

health of a community is the North Karelia project in Finland. In the 1960s, Finnish men had the highest death rate from heart disease in the world. North Karelia, in the east of the country, was particularly hard-hit. In 1972, the Finnish government, working with the World Health Organization, stepped in to help.

The problem was the North Karelian diet. North Karelia is a dairy farming area, and, consequently, the local people ate lots of high-fat dairy products such as butter, cream, whole milk, and cheese. They ate few fruits and vegetables; in fact, many people in the farming community felt that only cattle should eat green vegetables.

Doctors, nurses, teachers, social workers, and counselors were all trained to help the North Karelians adopt a more healthy lifestyle. Healthy eating practices were introduced at workplaces and schools; competitions encouraged people to lose weight with the help of nutrition experts; supermarkets were urged to promote the sale of fruit and vegetables. The farmers were also encouraged to grow crops of berries, which grow well in Finland, to supply the fruit that was so desperately needed in their diets.

The early results were so encouraging that in 1977, the project was extended to the whole of Finland. The North Karelia project ended in 1997. It was a spectacular success. The number of deaths from coronary heart disease dropped 82 percent. Life expectancy among men rose by eight years, from sixty-five to seventy-three.

WHAT WOULD YOU DO?

You Are in Charge
You are mayor of a city that has the highest levels of obesity in the whole country. You want to start up an equivalent of the North Karelia project. How are you going to plan the campaign? Who would you need to work with?

What would you do?

Consumption of fruit and vegetables climbed from the lowest in Europe to the highest in northern Europe. The project led to dietary changes throughout Finland. Between 1969 and 2002, deaths from chronic heart disease dropped 76 percent among Finnish men thirty-five to sixty-four years old.

Today, the World Health Organization uses the North Karelia project as a model for improving the health of communities. It has set up similar projects in other regions, including China, the Americas, and the Middle East. With effort on all sides, the obesity epidemic can be halted.

These patients are being weighed at a fat reduction hospital in China. The hospital aims to help people lose weight through a combination of diet, exercise, and acupuncture.

Glossary

anemia A condition in which someone does not have enough red blood cells or whose red blood cells do not contain enough hemoglobin (a protein containing iron), resulting in poor health

anorexia nervosa A life-threatening eating disorder that makes people so concerned about losing weight that they diet excessively

Body Mass Index (BMI) A measurement used to show whether someone is underweight, a normal weight, overweight, or obese

calorie A unit used to measure the energy contained within food and used by our bodies

Common Agricultural Policy (CAP) A policy of the European Union (EU) that determines what products may be farmed within the EU and how much farmers can be paid for their produce

developing country Also known as the Third World or the countries of the South, developing countries include all the regions of Africa, Asia (except for Japan), Latin America and the Caribbean, plus Melanesia, Micronesia, and Polynesia

dialysis A treatment that filters the waste products from the blood of patients whose kidneys are not functioning properly; it is done by a kidney dialysis machine

energy dense Describes certain foods such as potato chips and chocolate bars that contain many calories for their weight

estrogen A female sex hormone

insulin A hormone created by the pancreas that regulates the level of sugar in the blood

iron deficiency Inadequate iron in the body; this can lead to anemia when someone does not have enough red blood cells; meat and green leafy vegetables supply iron

metabolism The process by which a body absorbs food and converts it into energy

osteoarthritis A disease affecting the body's joints

testosterone A male sex hormone

vitamin A Also known as *retinol*, vitamin A is found in vegetables, egg yolk, and fish liver oil and is essential for growth

Further Information

Books

Critser, Greg. *Fat Land: How Americans Became the Fattest People in the World.* Penguin Books, 2004.

Dalton, Sharron. *Our Overweight Children: What Parents, Schools and Communities Can Do to Control the Fatness Epidemic.* University of California Press, 2004.

Lawrence, Felicity. *Not on the Label: What Really Goes into the Food on Your Plate.* Penguin Books, 2004.

Schlosser, Eric. *Fast Food Nation: The Dark Side of the All-American Meal.* Houghton Miflin, 2001.

Shanley, Ellen and Colleen Thompson. *Fueling the Teen Machine.* Bull Publishing, 2001.

Web Sites

American Diabetes Association
www.diabetes.org/home.jsp

American Obesity Association
www.obesity.org

BBC Online
www.bbc.co.uk/health/

Better Health Channel Australia
www.betterhealth.vic.gov.au

British Nutrition Foundation
www.nutrition.org.uk

Food and Agriculture Organization of the United Nations
www.fao.org

Food Standards Agency
www.foodstandards.gov.uk/
healthiereating

International Food Policy Research Institute
www.ifpri.org

National Obesity Forum
www.nationalobesityforum.org.uk

World Diabetes Foundation
www.worlddiabetesfoundation.org

World Health Organization
www.who.int/en

Publisher's note to educators and parents: Our editors have carefully reviewed these Web sites to ensure that they are suitable for children. Many Web sites change frequently, however, and we cannot guarantee that a site's future contents will continue to meet our high standards of quality and educational value. Be advised that children should be closely supervised whenever they access the Internet.

What Would You Do?

Page 10:

Doing nothing would put a burden on the health-care system in the country. Costs will go up, and people who develop diabetes may not be able to pay for their medicine. Business productivity will also be affected because of the many sick days caused by obesity-related health problems. The country's economy could suffer.

A national obesity and healthy eating awareness campaign can tackle the problem. Your government, however, will be competing with the advertising campaigns that producers of unhealthy foods run to persuade consumers to buy their food. Is the government prepared to invest the millions of dollars required to spread the healthy eating and lifestyle message?

Putting a tax on unhealthy food to discourage people from buying it may work, but what about providing consumers with inexpensive, healthy alternatives? Will the government come up with agricultural policies that encourage the cheap production of fruit and vegetables so that even the poorest people can afford them?

Page 16:

In this situation you could:

■ Reduce the fat in your products and promote this on the packaging.

■ Offer proof of purchase seals on the potato chip pakcages that people can collect to buy sports equipment for themselves or their schools.

■ Fund research into obesity and obesity-related problems.

■ Offer to fund healthy eating campaigns and work in conjunction with the government to encourage people to live healthy lives.

■ Make sure that you promote your company's good works to consumers through advertising. This is to ensure that your profits from potato chip sales do not drop because of the suggested link between your products and obesity.

Page 23:

You could ban candy, potato chips, and similar foods from vending machines at your school and from the cafeteria. You could also ban such foods from the premises, so that students would not be allowed to have them in packed lunches.

These solutions, however, may not be as simple as they sound. The consequences of a ban could be that the school would lose money. Vending machine sales are often used to supplement school funds. Extra staff would be needed to check all the children's lunch boxes and explain to parents why the food has been returned uneaten. This sort of action is likely to create some bad feeling.

An alternative policy could be to promote a healthy eating lifestyle to both children and parents through a series of workshops—for parents in the evening and for children during the school day. You could ensure that more healthy choices are offered in the cafeteria together with your healthy lifestyle education program and only offer healthy foods in vending machines.

Page 30:

You could take your children to a doctor to prescribe some exercise and some dietary and weight targets. You could find support groups that help young people who suffer from being overweight. The whole family could learn about healthy eating and then take part in shopping and cooking. A family keep-fit action plan could also help. This could include simple activities like walking to places whenever possible and some fun family activities at the local recreation center, too. Television time could be limited to two hours per day or used as a reward for exercising and eating well.

Page 37:

In developing countries, high levels of obesity are usually found in the cities. You could target city schools with a healthy eating message backed up by poster advertising campaigns on public transportation and billboards.

Obesity in developing countries is a new problem. Research and statistics are needed to get a true picture of how it is affecting your people. You could ask the World Health Organization to help set up a research program in your country. You could also meet with sugarcane industry officials and union representatives and explain the purpose behind your campaign. You could offer to work with them to develop new markets and uses for cane. You would also like them to investigate growing other, healthier crops for use within your country and for export. Your government could subsidize these crops.

Page 44:

You could start by calling a meeting with local doctors and health professionals and inviting them to express their views, ideas, and solutions to the problem. The issue should also be discussed with your local government representatives to make sure that they recognize the seriousness of the situation and are eager to help.

Such campaigns usually need additional funds and outside expertise. National governments and international organizations such as WHO and the United Nations may be able to help because they have significant experience in this area.

The project will involve people at all levels in your city —health professionals, educators, sports and recreation coaches, local stores, and, of course, the people themselves.

Index